The Dating Dad

Presence, Integrity, and Love After Divorce

Book 4 in The Present Dad Series

Brandon Antoni

Next Chapter Imprint

ISBN: 978-1-969552-04-5 (Paperback) Published by Next Chapter Imprint Printed in the United States of America First Edition

For my children — you are the reason, the anchor, and the inspiration behind every page.

And for every dad holding this book in his hands: you are not alone. This road may feel unfamiliar, heavy, or even impossible at times, but there is hope and strength ahead. You are more than your past, and your kids need the man you are becoming. May these words remind you that presence, healing, and integrity will always lead you forward — both as a father and as a man ready to love again.

Introduction

There is a moment — and most divorced dads know exactly what it feels like — when the dust of the separation starts to settle, the initial survival mode begins to lift, and you find yourself standing in your new life wondering, What now? The kids are asleep. The apartment is quiet. And you are somewhere between healing and hoping.

That is where this book begins.

The Dating Dad: Presence, Integrity, and Love After Divorce grew out of the same journey that inspired The Present Dad. That book was about showing up — for your children, in the middle of the chaos and grief of divorce, choosing to be present even when the ground was still shaking beneath you. This book picks up where that one left off. Because the journey does not end when you find your footing as a single dad. At some point, most of us start thinking about connection again. About companionship. About whether it is possible to love well after loss.

The answer is yes. But the road there matters as much as the destination.

The same principles that made you a better present dad — healing with intention, acting with integrity, leading with love rather than fear — apply to every step of the dating journey. This book is not a playbook for getting back out there as fast as possible. It is a roadmap from hurt to healing, from rushing to readiness, from loneliness to genuine, grounded connection.

If you have read The Present Dad, you will recognize the structure. Each chapter opens with a guiding quote, moves through honest reflection and practical tools, and closes with a story from the journey, real questions to sit with, and a concrete challenge to try during the week ahead. You can read front-to-back, or you can jump to the chapter that meets you where you are right now. If you are brand new to all of this, start at the beginning. If you are somewhere in the middle of the journey, find the chapter that speaks to your season.

This book is the fourth in The Present Dad Series. It follows The Present Dad and sits alongside In Their Own Voices, which explores what your children are experiencing through this transition. It also pairs with The Blended Dad, for those further down the road navigating the beautiful, complicated territory of building a new family. Each book stands on its own, but together they form a complete guide for the dad who refuses to disappear — who is determined to show up, heal up, and keep growing.

You are not damaged goods. You are not too far gone. And your kids are not doomed because their family looks different now. What they need more than anything is a dad who is honest enough to do the work, humble enough to ask for help, and brave enough to move forward with integrity.

That is the dad this book is written for.

That is you.

Let's get to work.

CHAPTER 1

Heal Before You Date

"Your kids don't need you to be dating — they need you to be steady."

The night I downloaded my first dating app after my divorce, I was sitting in the parking lot of a grocery store. It was a Friday. My kids were at their mom's for the weekend, and I had just bought a rotisserie chicken and a six-pack because I could not think of what else to do with myself. I sat in the car longer than I should have, phone in hand, scrolling through profile after profile. I told myself I was just looking. I told myself I was ready.

I was not ready. I was lonely, and those two things felt identical at the time.

That is the trap so many of us fall into after a divorce. The loneliness is real and it is heavy, and it does not take long before the idea of someone new — someone who looks at you like you matter, someone who laughs at your jokes, someone who makes the quiet stop — starts to feel like a solution. But loneliness is not the same as readiness, and the difference matters more than most of us realize when we are sitting in parking lots at nine o'clock on a Friday night.

Rushing back into dating does not heal the wound. It covers it. And covered wounds do not heal cleanly. They fester. They complicate every new relationship you try to build. They seep into your parenting — the distraction, the restlessness, the way your kids can sense that your attention is somewhere else even when you are physically in the room. Your children are perceptive in ways that still surprise me. They notice when you are present, and they notice when you are chasing something.

Here is what I learned the hard way: the work of healing is not glamorous, and it is not fast, and it does not feel like progress most of the time. I went to my first therapy session expecting the counselor to help me figure out how to navigate life as a single dad. Instead, the first real session turned the lens around. The questions were about me — my patterns, my wounds going further back than the marriage, the ways I had contributed to the breakdown of my relationship. I drove home feeling stripped down and a little hollowed out. It was humbling in the deepest sense of that word.

But it was also the most freeing thing I had done in years.

Healing is not the same as numbing. Numbing is the dating apps, the busyness, the nights you fill so completely that you never have to sit with the quiet. Healing is the harder thing — the therapy session that turns the mirror on you, the journal you actually write in even when what comes out makes you wince, the phone call to your brother where you finally say out loud how scared you are. Healing is choosing to feel the loss fully enough that it loses its grip on you, rather than letting it drive every decision you make for the next three years.

Your kids need you to do this work. Not because they are waiting for you to be perfect, but because they are watching. They are building their understanding of how adults handle pain, how men handle failure, how fathers rebuild. The steadiness you develop through real healing becomes the ground they stand on. And that steadiness — not a new partner, not a busier schedule — is what makes them feel safe.

Practical Ways to Heal Before You Date

- Start therapy with a licensed counselor who specializes in divorce and co-parenting. This is not a weakness — it is the most strategic thing you can do for yourself and your kids. Even six to eight sessions can shift everything.

- Journal consistently, even badly. You do not need to be a writer. Just write three sentences before bed: what you felt today, what you are grateful for, and one thing you want to release. The act of putting words to experience is itself a form of processing.
- Do the forgiveness work — all of it. That means your ex, yes. But it also means yourself. The guilt and shame that divorced dads carry can be paralyzing. Write a letter you never send. Speak it out loud in the car. Find a way to name the regret and then set it down.
- Build a rhythm for your solo weekends. When the kids are away, do not just survive the quiet — structure it intentionally. A morning run, a meal with a friend, a project around the apartment. Routine creates stability, and stability creates space for real healing.
- Measure readiness by peace, not time. Before you consider dating, ask yourself: Can I think about my ex without anger or grief flooding my chest? Can I spend a full day alone and feel okay? Can I talk about my divorce without it defining me? Readiness looks like peace — not perfect peace, but a real, working peace.

A Story from the Journey

I remember the night I realized I was not ready. Not the parking lot night — a different one, a few months later. I had matched with someone on an app who seemed genuinely great. We texted for a few days and she asked a simple question: What did you learn about yourself from your marriage? I stared at that question for a long time. I typed and deleted four different answers. Every version was either defensive or deflecting. I could not answer it honestly because I had not actually asked it honestly. I had been so focused on what had been done to me, on the ways the marriage had failed, that I had never really sat with my own part in it.

I did not respond that night. Instead, I closed the app and opened my journal for the first time in months. I wrote for an hour. It was not pretty. But it was real. And when I finally answered that question — weeks later, in therapy — it was the beginning of something that actually looked like healing.

Dad Reflection

- Are you pursuing dating because you feel ready, or because you feel lonely? Sit with the difference honestly.
- What unresolved emotions — anger, grief, guilt, shame — are you still carrying from the marriage and divorce? Have you brought them into the light, or are they still running quietly in the background?
- If your kids could describe your mood and presence over the past month, what would they say? What does that tell you about where you are right now?

Takeaways

- Loneliness is real, but it is not the same as readiness. Learn to tell the difference before you act.
- Rushing into dating covers the wound rather than healing it, and the cost shows up in your parenting and your future relationships.
- Real healing involves therapy, honest self-reflection, forgiveness work, and structured routine — none of it is fast, but all of it is worth it.
- Your kids are building their understanding of how adults handle pain by watching you. Your healing is a gift to them, not just to yourself.

Dad Challenge

This week, do one thing that is genuinely about healing rather than distraction. Book the therapy appointment you have been putting off. Write in a journal for twenty minutes without stopping. Call a trusted friend and say the thing out loud that you have been keeping to yourself. Choose one honest act of healing — and notice how different it feels from the things you normally reach for when the quiet gets loud.

CHAPTER 2

Your Kids Come First

"Your children don't need a replacement parent — they need your presence."

There is a version of post-divorce parenting that looks fine from the outside. Dad shows up for his days, the kids are fed and clothed and getting to school. But underneath, his attention is fractured — a phone full of notifications, a mind always partially somewhere else, weekends that pass in a haze of half-conversations and screens. His kids learn not to expect too much. They stop trying to tell him things. They get quiet in the particular way that children go quiet when they have learned that the full version of you is not really available.

I have been that dad. I am not proud of it, but I have been him.

The pull of new possibility is powerful. When you are starting to feel like yourself again — when someone is texting you good morning and making you laugh and reminding you that you are still interesting, still worth someone's attention — it is intoxicating. But your kids are watching where your attention goes. They always are. And every time they look up and you are somewhere else, something registers in them even if they never say a word about it.

Your children are not passengers in the story of your new life. They are the central characters. Before any new relationship can be healthy — for you, for the other person, or for your kids — your children need to feel that they are anchored. Not that they control your choices or that you will never have a life outside of them, but that you are theirs in the most fundamental way. That when they need you, you are there. That when the weekend comes, you are truly present.

I learned this during my daughter's second-grade music recital. I had a date that same evening — someone I had been talking to for two weeks, a first date I had been genuinely excited about. I had already told myself I would make the recital work around it. She was going on at six, I could be out by seven-thirty, and the date was at eight.

Then I watched her backstage, through a gap in the curtain, looking out at the audience before the show started. She was scanning every row. Looking for me. When she spotted me — not at seven-thirty, but right there in the third row with ten minutes to spare — her whole face changed. She straightened up. She smiled at the floor for a second, just to herself, and then looked back up.

I cancelled the date. I texted from the parking lot after the show. And that night, I found a folded piece of paper under my apartment door that she must have slipped through when I dropped her off. It said, in her handwriting: You came. I love you daddy. I kept that note. I keep it in my wallet still. It is the clearest reminder I have of what presence actually costs and what it actually gives.

When your children feel genuinely secure — when they know without a doubt that they are your priority — they are actually more resilient when change comes. They can handle the idea of Dad eventually dating someone because the foundation is solid. The security you build now does not disappear when a new relationship enters the picture. It expands. But you have to build it first, and you build it by showing up, again and again, even when something else is pulling at you.

Practical Ways to Put Your Kids First

- Create non-negotiable presence rituals. A bedtime routine, Saturday morning breakfast, a regular one-on-one activity with each child. These rituals signal to your kids that they have a standing reservation in your life that nothing cancels.
- Put the phone face-down during kid time. Not just during big events — during dinner, during homework help, during the car ride home from school. Physical presence without mental presence is not really presence.
- Check in with your kids about how they are doing — and mean it. Not the surface question, but the real one. "What was hard this week?" "Is there anything you've been thinking about?" Let them tell you without rushing to fix it.
- Do not introduce dating into your kids' world before it is serious. Keeping the two worlds separate in the early stages protects your children from unnecessary attachment and loss if a relationship does not work out.
- Let their schedule set the pace. If your child has a game, a recital, a school event, or just a hard week — that takes priority. Every time you choose them, it compounds. Presence is not one big gesture; it is a thousand small ones.

A Story from the Journey

There was a stretch of time after my divorce when I thought I was showing up but I was not really there. I was at the dinner table but I was thinking about messages I needed to send. I was at the park but I was mentally rehearsing conversations I needed to have. My son started telling me about something that happened at school one afternoon and I gave him a distracted "mm-hmm" and he just... stopped. He looked at me for a second, then looked at the floor, and changed the subject.

I caught it. Just barely, but I caught it.

I put my phone in my pocket. I said, "Hey — go back. Tell me what happened." He looked at me with this careful expression, like he was deciding whether to trust that I actually meant it. Then he told me the whole story. I listened. I laughed at the right part. I asked a follow-up question.

When we were done he said, "That's pretty good, right Dad?" and I said, "That's the best thing I've heard all day." He grinned. It cost me about four minutes. What it gave back was incalculable.

Dad Reflection

- Where does your attention actually go during your time with your kids? Be honest with yourself about the phone, the mental drift, the distracted presence.
- Do your children know, in concrete and demonstrated ways, that they are your priority? What is one thing you could do this week to make that clearer?
- How would your kids describe your presence on a typical evening or weekend? What would they say, and what does that tell you?

Takeaways

- Your children are the central characters in your story — not passengers. They need to feel anchored before any new relationship enters the picture.
- Kids notice where your attention goes, even when they do not say anything. Distracted presence sends a message.
- Non-negotiable rituals, real conversations, and physical presence with the phone put away build the security your kids need to eventually accept change.

- The investment you make in presence now creates the foundation that makes future transitions healthier for everyone.

Dad Challenge

This week, choose one moment with your kids where you are completely, phones-down, mentally-present with them. Not a special occasion — a normal evening. Dinner, a drive, homework time. Give them your full attention for that stretch, ask a real question, and listen to the whole answer. Notice what happens in the room when you are truly there. That is what they need. That is what you are capable of giving.

CHAPTER 3

Rebuilding Your Identity

"Before you can love someone else well, you need to know and love who you are."

Divorce does something disorienting to your sense of self that nobody really warns you about. For years, your identity was woven together with another person's. You were a husband. You were part of a unit. Your routines, your habits, your social circle, your sense of what your life looked like — all of it was built around a partnership. And then it is gone, and you are standing in the wreckage of a self that turns out to be less defined than you thought.

I noticed it in the strangest ways.

About three months after I moved into my apartment, I was driving alone on a Saturday and I turned off the podcast I had been listening to. The silence settled in, and I realized I had no idea what music I actually wanted to hear. I reached for the radio and scrolled and stopped and scrolled again. For a few minutes, I just sat there, genuinely unsure. Every song I considered, I was filtering through someone else's taste. My ex had opinions about music. I had adjusted to them so gradually that I had stopped noticing my own.

I ended up putting on a band I had loved in college — loud, a little chaotic, exactly the kind of music that had always made me feel something specific and good. I had not listened to them in years. I turned it up. And I drove for an hour just listening, and somewhere in that hour I thought: I missed this. I missed myself. That is what identity rebuilding feels like. Not a grand reinvention, not a dramatic transformation — just a slow reclamation of the things that were always yours. The music you actually love. The hobby you gave up because it did not fit the schedule or the dynamic. The friends you drifted from because couple-friendships had replaced individual ones. The version of yourself that existed before you became someone's husband, and that still exists now. waiting to be remembered.

This work matters for dating in a way that is not obvious at first. When you enter a new relationship without a clear sense of who you are, you do it all over again — the slow adjustment, the gradual accommodation, the identity drift. You end up in relationships that are wrong for you because you have no fixed point to navigate from. You choose based on who is available rather than who is right. You repeat the same patterns because the same unexamined version of yourself keeps making the same unexamined choices.

Your kids benefit from this work too, and not just abstractly. They benefit from seeing a dad who is alive — who has interests, who laughs genuinely, who is engaged in his own life rather than just managing logistics. Children borrow their sense of possibility from the adults around them. A dad who is actively becoming himself again, who is curious and present and engaged with life, shows his kids that adults can rebuild. That identity is not fixed. That the best version of yourself can be in progress and still be worth loving.

Practical Ways to Rebuild Your Identity

- Make a list of things you used to love that you let go. Hobbies, music, activities, types of people you used to spend time with. Pick one item and reintroduce it this month. Not as a project — just as a small act of reclamation.

- Get physically engaged with something. The gym, a hiking trail, a rec league, a martial arts class — something that puts you in your body. Physical engagement builds confidence and clarity in ways that are hard to replicate through mental work alone.

- Rebuild friendships outside the context of your marriage. Couple-friendships often dissolve after divorce. Invest in your own friendships — men who know you, who knew you before, who will speak honestly to you.
- Try things alone that you used to avoid. A restaurant, a movie, a concert, a weekend trip. Learning to enjoy your own company is not just a coping skill — it is a sign of genuine self-possession, and it is attractive.
- Notice what you think and feel without editing it through someone else's lens. In conversations, in preferences, in opinions. Practice saying what you actually think. The habit of self-erasure that sometimes develops in marriages takes time to unlearn.

A Story from the Journey

After the music-in-the-car moment, I started making small changes. I picked up a guitar that had been sitting in a case in my closet for the better part of six years. I was terrible. My fingers had forgotten everything. But I played for thirty minutes on a Tuesday night, alone in my apartment, and it felt like introducing myself to someone I had been missing.

A few months later, I signed up for a woodworking class at the local community center. I had always wanted to learn. In my marriage, it had never quite fit — the schedule, the expense, the space. In my apartment, with my Saturday mornings to myself, there was nothing to fit around. Just me, deciding what I wanted.

I was not great at woodworking either, at first. But I showed up every week. And when my son came to stay with me on weekends, I would show him what I was working on. He started asking questions. He wanted to try. One afternoon we worked on a small shelf together, badly, happily. He still has it in his room.

Rebuilding yourself is not just for you. It turns out to be a gift that lands in the most unexpected places.

Dad Reflection

- What parts of your identity got lost or eroded during your marriage? Are you beginning to reclaim them, or are they still sitting in a closet somewhere?
- What do you actually like — not what you have been conditioned to like or what fits the image you project, but what genuinely lights you up? Can you name three things?
- What do you want your kids to see when they look at you? Are you becoming that version of yourself? What would it take to move one step closer?

Takeaways

- Divorce strips away identity in gradual, disorienting ways. Rebuilding it is not dramatic — it is a series of small reclamations.
- Without a clear sense of self, dating leads to the same patterns and the same drift. Identity is the compass that guides you toward relationships that actually fit.
- Physical engagement, reclaimed hobbies, honest friendships, and the practice of your own opinions all build the self-knowledge you need to date well.
- A dad who is actively, visibly alive and becoming himself models something powerful for his children — the possibility of rebuilding, and the dignity of becoming.

Dad Challenge

This week, do one thing that is purely about reclaiming you. Listen to the music you actually love. Pull out the gear from the hobby you abandoned. Call the friend you lost touch with. Take yourself somewhere alone, without your phone as a companion, and just be there. Notice what comes up. Notice what it feels like to be a person with your own inner life again. That person is who your next relationship will fall in love with — and he is worth knowing first.

CHAPTER 4

The Right Reasons to Date

"The best relationships start when you're ready to give love, not when you're desperate to receive it."

Motives matter. Not just morally — strategically, practically, in ways that determine whether a relationship ends up being life-giving or quietly draining. The problem is that most of us do not examine our motives when we start dating again. We just feel the pull and follow it, telling ourselves a simple story: I am ready, I am lonely, I deserve happiness. And all of that may be true. But it is not the whole story.

I had to sit with my own motives, and what I found was uncomfortable.

About four months after my divorce was finalized, I created a dating profile. I told myself it was about connection — that I was healed enough, ready enough, that it was time. But when I actually sat with the honest question of why — not the polished answer, but the real one — what came up was this: I wanted to prove something to my ex. I wanted her to see that I was fine. More than fine. I wanted her to hear through mutual friends that I was dating someone interesting, someone who thought I was worth choosing. I wanted, if I am being totally honest, to win.

That is a terrible reason to bring another human being into your life.

And it is a common one. We date after divorce because we are lonely — that is real. But we also date to recover our pride. To prove our desirability.

To quiet the voice that wonders if the divorce was evidence of something fundamentally unlovable in us. We date to fill a hole, to escape the silence, to feel young again, to have someone take our side for once. None of these are reasons to build a relationship on. They are reasons to work through first.

The right reasons look different. They are quieter and steadier. They look like: I am genuinely enjoying my own life, and I would like to share it with someone. They look like: I have done enough healing that I can bring my whole self to a relationship, not just my need. They look like: I am not running from something — I am moving toward something. The difference is not about how long you have been divorced or how many therapy sessions you have had. It is about what is driving you.

Dating from a place of wholeness — even imperfect, still-in-progress wholeness — produces a completely different experience than dating from a place of desperation or proving. You make different choices. You tolerate different things. You communicate differently. You attract differently. When you are trying to get something from a relationship rather than bring something to it, that dynamic shapes everything from the first conversation forward.

Your kids feel the difference too, even if they cannot name it. A dad who is dating from steadiness looks different than a dad who is dating from frantic need. One is a man building something. The other is a man running from something. Your children need the former.

Practical Ways to Date from the Right Reasons

- Write down your honest "why." Not the polished version — the real one. Put it on paper and look at it. If you find ego, fear, loneliness, or revenge in there, do not judge yourself. Just name it. You cannot correct what you will not admit.

- Ask yourself whether you would be okay if you did not meet anyone new for the next six months. If the answer is no — if the idea of being alone that long feels genuinely unbearable — that is information about readiness, not a judgment of your character.

- Check what you are hoping dating will fix. If the list includes: feeling better about yourself, proving something to your ex, not having to be alone anymore — those are things healing should address, not dating.
- Notice whether you are excited about people or excited about the idea of having someone. One is readiness; the other is need. There is a real difference.
- Talk it through with someone who will tell you the truth. Your therapist. A trusted friend. Someone who will not just tell you what you want to hear. External perspective on your motives can save you from a lot of pain.

A Story from the Journey

I made myself sit with that question — Why do I want to date right now? — for a week before I answered it honestly. I journaled about it. I brought it to therapy. And the version I eventually wrote down was hard to look at: I wanted to prove I was still desirable. I wanted to feel chosen. I wanted to shove something in the face of the fear that the divorce had revealed some fundamental flaw in me.

That was not a reason to start dating. That was a reason to keep doing the work.

So I waited. I kept going to the gym. I kept going to my sessions. I started that woodworking class. I took my son on a camping trip. I called old friends I had let drift. I started actually enjoying my life in small, real ways.

And then one morning I woke up and the thought that came was different. Not I need to find someone. It was something closer to: My life is good. I would love to share it with the right person someday. That is when I created a profile. Not to prove anything, not to fill a void — just to be open. The difference in those two starting points changed everything about how I showed up.

Dad Reflection

- If you wrote down your honest reasons for wanting to date right now, what would they be? What percentage of those reasons are about giving, and what percentage are about getting?
- What do you hope a new relationship will fix or fill? Are those things that dating can actually address, or are they things healing needs to address first?
- What would it look like to date from a place of steadiness and surplus rather than need? What would you do differently?

Takeaways

- Motives shape everything — who you choose, how you show up, what you tolerate, what you create. Wrong motives produce painful patterns no matter who you are dating.
- Common wrong reasons: loneliness, ego, fear of being alone, proving something to an ex. Common right reasons: wholeness, genuine desire to share a good life, willingness to move slowly.
- The question is not just "Am I ready?" but "Why do I want this?" If you cannot answer honestly, you have more work to do first.
- Dating from a place of surplus — where you have something to give rather than something to get — is visible to your kids, your dates, and yourself. It changes the entire trajectory.

Dad Challenge

This week, write a private, unfiltered answer to this question: Why do I want to date right now? No editing for how it sounds. Just write the truth. Then sit with what you find. If you see wholeness and genuine readiness, that is worth celebrating. If you see fear, pride, or need, do not use it as a reason to shame yourself — use it as a road map for the work that still remains. Honesty before action is always the braver choice.

CHAPTER 5

Confidence Without Ego

"True confidence isn't about proving yourself — it's about knowing yourself."

Re-entering the dating world after years of marriage is one of the stranger experiences a man can have. You were off the market for a decade, maybe longer. The world changed while you were in it. The apps are different. The language is different. The pace is different. And you are different — older, more tired in some ways, more real in others. The version of yourself that first got into a relationship does not map cleanly onto the man standing here now.

That gap — between who you were and who you are, between the dating world you remember and the one that currently exists — can make even a confident man feel like a teenager again. And there is a temptation, when you feel that uncertain, to overcompensate. To come in louder than you actually are. To perform a version of yourself that feels more impressive than the real one. To brag a little, posture a little, project a level of togetherness that is slightly ahead of where you actually live.

I did this on my first real date after my divorce. I talked too much. I name-dropped things about my career. I made the conversation about impressing her rather than knowing her. By the end of the evening I had successfully presented a polished highlight reel of myself and learned almost nothing about who she was. On the drive home I felt vaguely hollow, like I had aced an audition for a role I did not actually want to play.

The second date I had — with someone different, a few months later — I came in differently. I was tired that week, honestly. My son had been sick, I had missed a deadline at work, and I showed up to that dinner table as exactly who I was: a man doing his best, interested in a real conversation, genuinely curious about this person. I said at some point in the evening, "I'm still figuring out what this whole thing looks like — the dating part, the co-parenting part, all of it. But I'm figuring it out on purpose."

She said that was the most honest thing anyone had said to her in months. We talked for three hours.

Real confidence is not the absence of insecurity. It is the decision not to be run by it. It is the willingness to sit down across from a stranger and say, in effect: I know who I am. I am still becoming who I want to be. And I am not afraid for you to see both of those things. That is not swagger. That is not bravado. It is groundedness, and it is far more attractive than performance.

Your kids need to see this, too. Children who watch their dad perform — who sense that the version of Dad in front of company is different from the one at home — learn something subtle and damaging about authenticity. But kids who see a dad who is comfortable in his own skin, who can say "I don't know" without embarrassment and "I was wrong" without crumbling — those kids are learning something foundational about real self-respect.

Confidence without ego means you are not trying to win the date. You are trying to find out whether this person and this version of you are a genuine fit. That is a completely different game, and it is one you can play honestly from the first conversation.

Practical Ways to Build Confidence Without Ego

- Know your own story. Be able to talk about your divorce honestly, briefly, and without bitterness. A man who can describe a painful chapter of his life with clarity and grace is a man who has done real work — and it shows.

- Ask more questions than you answer. Real confidence does not need to fill all the space. Genuine curiosity — the kind where you actually listen to the response — is more attractive than a performance of impressive.

- Be honest about where you are. You do not need to lead with everything, but do not manufacture a more polished version of your life than actually exists. The right person will be drawn to your realness, not repelled by it.

- Acknowledge what you do not know. About dating, about yourself, about what you are looking for. "I'm still figuring that out" is a confident answer when it is true.

- Let your kids see your real confidence. Let them see you handle hard conversations calmly, own your mistakes without drama, and move through uncertainty without panicking. That is the version of confidence worth modeling.

A Story from the Journey

I had a friend watch me prepare for that first date. He saw me change my outfit three times. He watched me rehearse a few things I wanted to say. He finally looked at me and said: "You know what women find more attractive than a guy who has it all together? A guy who is honest about the fact that he doesn't."

I thought he was trying to make me feel better. He was not. He was telling me a true thing that I was not ready to hear yet.

I learned it the hard way — that first date, with all the performance. And then I learned it in the best possible way — that second one, where I showed up as myself and had the best conversation I had experienced in years. The difference was not what I wore or what I said. The difference was which version of me walked in the door.

Walk in as yourself. That is the whole strategy.

Dad Reflection

- Where does your confidence come from right now — your actual sense of self, or external validation and performance? Be honest about the answer.
- Think about a time when you felt genuinely confident — not impressive, but comfortable. What was different about that moment? How do you recreate it?
- What would it look like to show your kids real confidence rather than performed confidence this week?

Takeaways

- The gap between your married self and your current self can trigger overcompensation — performance, posturing, bravado. Recognize it for what it is.
- Real confidence is groundedness, not swagger. It is the willingness to be seen as you actually are, without apology but without performance.
- Asking real questions, being honest about your story, and acknowledging uncertainty are all acts of genuine confidence — and they create actual connection.
- The version of yourself that is real and in-progress is more attractive, more trustworthy, and more worth building on than any highlight reel.

Dad Challenge

This week, practice confidence in a low-stakes situation. Have one conversation — with a neighbor, a colleague, someone at school pickup — where you say something honest and real rather than impressive. Notice what it feels like to be received well for the unpolished version of you. That is the person worth bringing to a date. That is the man worth knowing. Practice being him before it matters.

CHAPTER 6

Modern Dating for Dads

"The dating world has changed — but the values that build love haven't."

I want to tell you about the first week I was seriously on the apps.

I downloaded two of the big ones. I spent an embarrassing amount of time on my profile — photos, bio, the whole thing. And then I dove in. Swiping. Matching. Texting. Within forty-eight hours I had more conversations going simultaneously than I had ever managed in my life, most of them going nowhere, several of them fizzling after a few exchanges, one of them suddenly stopping mid-conversation with no explanation and no contact again.

I was exhausted. And I had not even been on a date yet.

Welcome to modern dating.

The landscape has changed dramatically since most of us were last in it. Dating apps have restructured everything — how people meet, how they communicate, what they expect from the early stages of connection. There is a gamification to it that is genuinely hard to resist. The dopamine hit of a new match, the quick texting that never quite goes anywhere, the swiping that starts to feel like channel surfing rather than searching for a human being. It is efficient and simultaneously deeply inefficient, and for a dad who is already managing a full life, it can become a second job that produces very little return.

Here is what I figured out over time: the apps are a tool, not a world. Used right — with limited time, clear intentions, and reasonable expectations — they can be a useful way to meet people you would never otherwise encounter. Used wrong, they become a way to spend your free time feeling simultaneously busy and lonely, watching potential connections disappear into the digital ether while the actual texture of your life goes unlived.

The thing is, the fundamentals have not changed. People still connect over shared experiences. They still trust what they see over time, not just what reads well in a bio. Humor, kindness, genuine interest in another person — these things still work the way they have always worked. The medium is new. The human part is not.

After about two months on the apps — feeling increasingly drained and increasingly hollow — I did something that turned out to change everything. I signed up for a community hiking group. Not as a dating strategy, just because I wanted to get outside more and I was tired of doing it alone. I showed up on a Saturday morning, slightly awkward, genuinely there for the hike.

Over the next few weeks, I met people. Real conversations on real trails, where you learn something about a person by whether they hold the door of an incline for the person behind them, by how they talk about their week, by whether they laugh at the right moments. I was not performing. I was just there.

That is where I met someone I eventually dated for several months. Not from a curated profile — from a muddy trail on a Saturday. The connection was easy in the way that only in-person connections can be easy, because it was built out of actual shared experience rather than constructed presentation.

Balance is the word I keep coming back to. Use the tools — they are real and they work for a lot of people. But do not let them own your time or your self-worth. And do not forget that the world outside your phone is full of real people living real lives, and some of those people are going to be far more interesting to you than any profile you ever swiped on.

Practical Ways to Navigate Modern Dating

- Set a time limit on app use. Twenty to thirty minutes a day, max. Beyond that, the returns diminish and the toll on your mood and time compounds. Apps are a tool, not a lifestyle.
- Do not let your match count or your message response rate define your worth. Algorithms and aesthetics filter people out for reasons that have nothing to do with your actual value as a human being. Do not internalize the numbers.
- Pursue at least one offline avenue simultaneously. A community group, a class, a sport, a volunteer opportunity. Shared experience creates real connection faster than any text exchange. Go be somewhere in the world with other people.
- Be honest in your profile about being a dad. Do not bury it or minimize it. Your children are part of your life — the right person will see that as a feature, not a bug. Lead with it without leading with every detail of your custody arrangement.
- Move from texting to real life relatively quickly. Long text chains rarely predict how a real conversation will go. Suggest a coffee or a walk within a week. Real connection happens in real time.

A Story from the Journey

About six weeks into my app experiment, I was sitting at my kitchen table on a Thursday night, phone in hand, managing four different conversations, enjoying none of them. My son was in the next room doing homework. At some point he called out, "Dad, can you help me with this?" and I said, "Just a minute" — and then twenty minutes passed before I got up.

He had figured it out himself by then. He did not say anything about it. But I caught myself sitting there with a phone full of conversations that meant nothing and a son in the next room who meant everything, and I felt it — the precise wrong ratio of attention.

I put the phone down. I went and sat next to him. The conversations could wait. The apps could wait. The whole project could wait.

The next Saturday I showed up to that hiking group for the first time. I left my phone in my jacket pocket. I talked to actual humans. I came home tired in a way that felt good rather than depleted.

The balance was right after that. The apps stayed, but they stayed in their lane.

Dad Reflection

- How much time are you currently spending on dating apps, and how does that time make you feel — energized or drained? Is the ratio worth it?
- Are you pursuing connection in the physical world — through community, activity, and shared experience — or are you primarily relying on digital channels? What would it take to add at least one offline avenue?
- How do you want your kids to experience your dating life — as invisible, as a distraction, or as a background reality that does not disrupt what they can rely on? What would it take to land in that third category?

Takeaways

- Dating apps are a tool, not a world. Used with clear limits and realistic expectations, they can be valuable. Used without limits, they become draining and distorting.

- The fundamentals of human connection — shared experience, genuine curiosity, humor, and showing up consistently — have not changed, regardless of the medium.
- Offline community and shared activity create real connection in ways that texting rarely can. Balance digital and in-person opportunities.
- Being honest about being a dad, moving to real life quickly, and limiting app time are practical strategies that will make your dating life more sustainable and more rewarding.

Dad Challenge

This week, choose one thing to change about how you are using dating technology. Delete one of the apps you check compulsively but rarely enjoy. Set a thirty-minute daily limit on the ones you keep. Sign up for one offline activity — a class, a community group, a sport, a volunteer opportunity. Make one move toward connection that does not require a swipe. Notice how it feels to pursue human connection in a way that also fills your life rather than draining it.

End of First Half The Dating Dad: Presence, Integrity, and Love After Divorce By Brandon Antoni Next Chapter Imprint — Book 4 in The Present Dad Series

CHAPTER 7

Timing, Boundaries, and Introductions

"Healthy relationships grow when you honor both your limits and your children's needs."

There's a question I used to get wrong every single time: When do I tell her I have kids? My instinct was to wait — to get through a date or two, see if there was something real there, and then drop the information like a confession. I thought I was being strategic. What I was actually being was avoidant. I was treating one of the most important parts of my identity as a liability instead of a truth.

The answer, I've come to learn, is simple: you tell her you're a dad early. Not on the first text, not in your opening message — but before you ever meet in person, she should know. It's not a confession. It's context. It's who you are. And if knowing you're a father is a dealbreaker for someone, you want to know that before you've invested time, energy, and hope into something that was never going to work anyway. Leading with your truth isn't a risk — it protects you both.

But knowing when to disclose that you're a dad is only one piece of the puzzle. The harder question — the one that took me much longer to get right — is when to introduce the person you're dating to your kids. And here's what I can tell you from painful, personal experience: there is no universal timeline, but there is a universal standard. You wait until the relationship has shown real, consistent stability. Not a month. Not because things are going great. You wait until you genuinely believe this person is going to be around, until you've seen who they are when they're tired, when they're frustrated, when life isn't convenient. Only then do you consider making that introduction.

Kids don't understand "we're just seeing how things go." When you bring someone into their world, they start to attach. And if that person disappears — even if it's mutual, even if it's gentle — your kids feel another loss. As a divorced dad, you know what loss feels like to them. Don't underestimate how much they're already carrying. Protecting them from unnecessary instability isn't overprotective — it's loving. Boundaries around introductions aren't about distrust; they're about respect for the emotional weight your children are already managing.

When the time does come, preparation matters. Don't spring it on them. Have a conversation first — calm, low-key, no big buildup. "There's someone I've been spending time with. She's kind, and I think you might like her. We're going to get lunch together sometime." That's it. No pressure, no performance. The first meeting should be something neutral and easy — a pizza place, a park, something that doesn't carry the weight of a formal introduction. Watch how everyone does. Pay attention to your kids' comfort. Pay attention to how she handles the moment. And go slowly.

The pace should feel safe for everyone — you, your kids, and the person you're dating. If she's the right woman, she will understand why you're moving carefully. She won't push for faster access to your children. She won't feel threatened by your protective instinct. And she'll be patient — not because you asked her to be, but because she genuinely respects what you're building. That patience is one of the earliest green lights you can watch for.

Practical Ways to Honor Timing and Boundaries

- Disclose that you're a dad before the first date. It shouldn't feel like a reveal — it's simply who you are. Lead with it.
- Set a personal benchmark for introductions. Many dads use six months of consistent dating as a minimum. Whatever your benchmark, know it before you're in the heat of a new relationship.
- Prepare your kids with age-appropriate conversations. A 7-year-old and a 14-year-old need different levels of information. Tailor the talk to where they are.
- Keep first meetings short, casual, and pressure-free. A one-hour outing with no agenda is far better than an all-day event with emotional weight behind it.
- Check in with your kids afterward. Ask how they felt. Listen without defensiveness. Their comfort matters, and their honesty is data you need.

A Story from the Journey

Early in my dating life after the divorce, I made the classic mistake. I was about four months into seeing someone, and things felt really good — fun, easy, consistent. I told myself that was enough. I introduced her to my kids on a Sunday afternoon at the park. My son was polite. My daughter was quiet in a way that told me she wasn't sure what to do with this information. Within six weeks, that relationship had ended for reasons that had nothing to do with my kids. But the fallout landed squarely on them. My daughter asked me one night, out of nowhere, "Is she coming back?" I didn't have a good answer.

The second time around, I waited. I waited until I was genuinely certain — not just hopeful, but certain — that the person I was with was someone stable and kind who understood what she was stepping into. When that introduction finally happened, it was low-key and quiet. Lunch, nothing fancy. My kids were relaxed. She was warm without being performative. Afterward, my son said, "She seems cool, Dad." That was it. No drama, no confusion, no questions I couldn't answer. Patience didn't just protect my kids — it made the moment better for all of us.

Dad Reflection

- Have I been honest with the women I've dated about the role my kids play in my life, or have I downplayed it to keep things simpler?
- What would need to be true about a relationship before I'd feel genuinely ready to introduce someone to my children?
- How have I prepared my kids — emotionally and practically — for the reality that I might date again?

Takeaways

- Disclosing that you're a dad early is not a liability — it's integrity in action.
- Children attach quickly, and early introductions can create painful losses if the relationship doesn't last.
- There is no universal timeline for introductions, but stability and consistency are the standard — not duration or chemistry.
- The right partner will respect your protective boundaries and match your patience.

Dad Challenge

This week, write down your personal guidelines for introductions — not someone else's rules, yours. How long do you want to wait? What would need to be true about the relationship? What would the first meeting look like? Having clarity before you're in the middle of a relationship means you make that decision from wisdom, not emotion.

CHAPTER 8

Dating with Integrity

"Integrity means showing up as the same man in private that you present in public."

There's a version of yourself you can perform on a date. You probably know the one — edited, polished, strategically curated. You mention the gym but not the bad month you had. You talk about how close you are with your kids, but you skip the part about the custody schedule that sometimes leaves you feeling hollow. You present the highlight reel and keep the rough cuts to yourself. For a night or two, it works. And then it starts to cost you.

Integrity in dating isn't about confessing everything on night one. It's about alignment — making sure the man you present on dates is recognizably the same man who shows up at 7 AM on a Tuesday. It means your words and your actions point in the same direction. It means you don't promise time you don't have, commitment you're not ready for, or a version of yourself you're still working to become. Integrity isn't perfection. It's honesty about where you actually are.

For divorced dads, one of the most common integrity failures is subtle. It's not lying exactly — it's minimizing. I used to mention my kids as an afterthought. I'd slip them in after I'd already built some rapport, like I was hoping the connection we'd made would soften the landing. I convinced myself I was being strategic, but what I was actually doing was treating my kids — the most important people in my life — as a potential obstacle rather than a central fact. And the women who couldn't handle it? Better to know that on date one than date ten.

When you lead with the truth — calmly, confidently, without apology — something shifts. The conversations become more real. The women who respond well are the ones who were worth talking to in the first place. And you stop wasting time on mismatches. That shift happened for me, and it changed everything. Not because honesty is magic, but because honesty is a filter. It clears the field and leaves you with the people who actually see you clearly and still want to be there.

Integrity also means respecting her story. She has a history too — relationships that didn't work, healing she's doing, questions she's asking herself. You want her to see you clearly; make sure you're returning the same generous attention. Don't steamroll her experience with your own narrative. Don't turn every conversation back to your divorce, your schedule, your kids. She is a whole person with a whole life. Treat her that way. That reciprocity — that mutual respect for each other's full humanity — is where real connection begins.

And finally: don't overpromise. It is tempting, especially when things are going well, to say things like "I'll make time" when you're not sure you can, or "I'll call every night" when your week already has three commitments and a custody handoff. Say what you mean and mean what you say. A woman who is genuinely right for you will understand the honest version of your life. She doesn't need the inflated version. And the man your kids need you to be — steady, trustworthy, consistent — is exactly the man you should bring to the table in dating too.

Practical Ways to Date with Integrity

- Lead with the fact that you're a dad. Make it the first significant thing she knows about you, not the last thing you reluctantly mention.
- Only promise what you can actually deliver. If your schedule is complicated, say so early — and let her decide if she can work with it.

- Share your real self, not a performance. Authenticity invites authenticity. The more honest you are, the more honest the connection becomes.
- Respect her time and her story. She has history too. Ask questions. Listen. Don't make every conversation about your journey.
- Check your motivations. Before a date, ask yourself: Am I showing up to find a genuine connection, or am I performing for approval? The difference matters.

A Story from the Journey

I cringe a little thinking about the first few dates I went on after the divorce. I had a whole system. I'd get through the first drink before I mentioned my kids. Sometimes two. I figured if she liked me enough by then, the kids wouldn't feel like a big deal. What I actually communicated, without saying it, was that my children were something to be managed around, not a core part of who I was.

One night, a woman I'd been seeing for about a month looked at me across the table and said, "I feel like you're still figuring out how much to let me see." She wasn't wrong. After that, I decided to change. The next time I was on a first date, I mentioned my kids in the first ten minutes. Not in a heavy way — just naturally, the way you mention anything that matters. "I have two kids — a son and a daughter. They're the center of my world." The woman across from me smiled and said, "Tell me about them." That was a completely different kind of beginning. And it turned out to be a much better kind of story.

Dad Reflection

- In what ways have I presented a "polished" version of myself that doesn't fully match the reality of my day-to-day life as a dad?

- Have I been overpromising in any area — time, availability, emotional readiness — because I want to impress rather than be honest?
- How do I want the women I date to see my fatherhood — as context for who I am, or as a complication I manage around them?

Takeaways

- Integrity in dating is alignment between who you are and how you present yourself — not confessing everything, but not hiding what matters.
- Minimizing your role as a dad to keep things comfortable is a subtle but real integrity failure.
- Leading with honesty filters out mismatches early and creates the conditions for genuine connection.
- Overpromising what you can't deliver undermines trust — even when the intentions behind it are good.

Dad Challenge

Before your next date — or right now if you're between them — write down five true things about your life that you sometimes downplay or save for later. Then ask yourself: what would it feel like to say these things plainly, without apology, on a first date? Practice saying them out loud. Honesty gets easier the more you do it, and the right person will thank you for it.

CHAPTER 9

Empathy and Communication

"Great relationships aren't built on charm or chemistry — they're built on understanding."

Chemistry gets all the credit. We talk about it like it's the whole story — that electric pull on a first date, the easy laughter, the sense that conversation just flows. And yes, chemistry matters. But chemistry without communication is a campfire in a windstorm. Bright for a moment, then gone. The relationships that last — the ones that actually become something — are built on the quieter work of learning to understand another person and letting them understand you.

Empathy is the foundation of that work. It is the practice of seeing the world through someone else's eyes, sitting with their experience long enough to understand it — not just tolerate it. After divorce, empathy can feel like a muscle you've let atrophy. You've been hurt. You've protected yourself. You've learned to be a little guarded, and that guardedness made sense. But guarded people build walls, and walls keep out pain and connection in equal measure. The work of dating again means slowly, deliberately letting some of those walls come down.

I know what it looks like when empathy breaks down in a relationship, because I lived it. During my marriage, hard conversations made me go quiet.

When things got tense, I'd shut down — not out of malice, but because I didn't know what else to do. I had never learned how to stay present in conflict. My response to emotional discomfort was to leave the room, metaphorically or literally. And that silence communicated something, even when I thought I was just avoiding a fight. It communicated: your feelings aren't safe with me. After the divorce, I made a decision. I was going to learn how to stay in hard conversations. Not perfectly — I still struggle — but I was going to try. And the trying made all the difference. I remember an early moment in a relationship after the divorce when we hit a wall. Something I said landed wrong, and she was hurt. The old me would have gotten defensive or shut down. Instead, I said, "I don't really know how to talk about this, but I want to try." That was it. No eloquent speech, no perfectly chosen words. Just a statement of honest intention. She relaxed. The conversation opened up. Something real happened between us that night, and it only happened because I stayed in the room.

Communication is how empathy becomes action. It is how you tell someone what you need without making them feel attacked. It is how you receive feedback without collapsing into defensiveness. Practical tools help: ask open-ended questions instead of ones that invite a simple yes or no. When she's talking, actually listen — not just waiting for your turn. Name what you're hearing: "It sounds like that felt dismissive to you." Those small practices signal that you're paying attention, that her experience matters to you, that you're not just here for the easy parts.

And here's the gift you might not expect: the empathy and communication you build in your dating life will show up in your parenting too. Your kids will notice. You will become a better listener, a calmer presence, someone who stays in the room when things get hard. Those skills don't live in just one relationship — they become part of who you are. My teenage daughter told me once, out of nowhere, "You actually listen to me now, Dad." I almost had to pull over. That was everything.

Practical Ways to Build Empathy and Communication

- Practice active listening. When she's speaking, put your phone away, make eye contact, and focus entirely on what she's saying — not your response.
- Ask open-ended questions. "How did that make you feel?" opens a door that "Were you upset?" closes.
- Name what you're hearing. Reflecting back what someone says — "It sounds like you felt overlooked" — confirms that you understood, not just heard.
- Stay in hard conversations. When you feel the urge to shut down or walk away, try saying: "I'm finding this hard to talk about, but I don't want to leave it." That honesty is a bridge.
- Extend the same empathy to your kids. Use every hard parenting conversation as practice. Your children are teaching you how to communicate, even when it doesn't feel that way.

A Story from the Journey

For most of my marriage, I was someone who left the room. Not always physically — but emotionally, I checked out when conversations got heavy. I had convinced myself I was keeping the peace. What I was actually doing was teaching the people I loved that my silence was the ceiling — that there was a limit to how deeply I'd engage.

After the divorce, I started pushing myself. A therapist once told me that staying present in a hard conversation is an act of love, and I kept that. One night, sitting across from someone I was falling for, we hit a rough patch of conversation — something I'd said had hurt her. I felt that old pull to deflect, to minimize. Instead, I took a breath and said, "I don't know how to talk about this, but I want to try." She looked at me differently after that. The conversation became something I was grateful we had. Months later, on a drive home from school, my daughter said it — "You actually listen to me now, Dad." I didn't say anything back. I just kept driving and let that land.

Dad Reflection

- When conversations get hard or emotional, what is my default response? Do I stay present or find a way to exit?
- Have I been practicing active listening — really listening — with the people who matter most to me?
- How has my communication in adult relationships shown up in how I communicate with my kids?

Takeaways

- Chemistry gets the credit, but empathy and communication do the actual work of building lasting relationships.
- After divorce, the tendency toward emotional guardedness is understandable — but walls don't discriminate between pain and connection.
- Staying in hard conversations, even imperfectly, communicates that the other person's experience matters to you.
- The communication skills you develop in dating show up in parenting — your kids will notice and benefit.

Dad Challenge

This week, pick one conversation you've been avoiding — with someone you're dating, a co-parent, or one of your kids — and decide to stay in it. You don't need the perfect words. Start with honest intention: "This is hard for me to talk about, but I don't want to leave it." Say that, and see what opens up.

CHAPTER 10

Red Flags and Green Lights

"Paying attention early can save you and your kids from heartache later."

Chemistry is a liar. Not always, not intentionally — but it clouds your vision at exactly the moment you need to see most clearly. There is no feeling in early dating quite like the pull of someone who lights you up, and that feeling has cost me more than I want to admit. When you are drawn to someone, you want to believe the best about them. You rationalize the things that don't sit right. You tell yourself it's too early to judge. And then, weeks or months in, you're sitting with the consequences of things you noticed but chose not to see.

As a divorced dad, you cannot afford to navigate by chemistry alone. You have more at stake than your own heart. Your kids are watching, even when they aren't in the room — they feel the shifts in your mood, your availability, your energy. They will eventually meet the person you've been spending time with. And even if they never do, the way a relationship affects you affects them. That raises the bar for who you let in. Not impossibly high — just honestly calibrated.

Red flags in a relationship are patterns, not isolated moments. Everyone has a bad day. What you're watching for is the consistent shape of someone's character. Pay attention when she dismisses your role as a dad — when fatherhood is treated as inconvenient or secondary rather than foundational to who you are. Watch for someone who pushes for fast commitment before the relationship has earned it, who tries to accelerate past the natural pace of trust-building. Notice if she's controlling — over your time, your decisions, your boundaries. Look at how she treats other people: waitstaff, strangers, your children if she's met them. Character shows up in small, unguarded moments.

And then there are green lights — the signs that tell you this is someone worth trusting with your full life. She respects your fatherhood, not as an obstacle she's patient with, but as something she genuinely values. She communicates openly, even when it's uncomfortable. She shows patience — not as a performance, but as a pattern. She holds herself accountable when she gets something wrong. Her values align with yours in the ways that actually matter: how she treats people, what she believes about family, what kind of future she's building toward. When you see these things consistently, that's not chemistry talking — that's character.

The question that helped me most was not "Do I like her?" I always liked the wrong ones too. The better question was: "Is this good for me and my kids?" Not just now, in the warmth of new attraction, but in six months, in a year, when life is ordinary and hard. Asking that question forces you to engage your mind as well as your heart, and for a divorced dad re-entering the dating world, that integration — head and heart working together — is one of the most important things you can cultivate.

Don't let urgency override wisdom. You're not running out of time. You're not desperate. You are a grown man who has been through something hard and come out the other side with clarity about what matters. Trust that clarity. Use it.

Practical Ways to Recognize Red Flags and Green Lights

- Watch the pattern, not the moment. One off night tells you very little. Three months of consistent behavior tells you nearly everything.

- Notice how she talks about your kids. Does she ask about them with genuine interest? Does she treat their existence as a natural and welcome part of your life?
- Pay attention to how she handles conflict. Does she take accountability? Stay calm? Come back to resolution? Or does she escalate, withdraw, or deflect?
- Ask yourself the hard question early. "Is this good for me and my kids?" is a better filter than "Do I like her?" — especially when chemistry is high.
- Trust your gut, but verify with your head. Your intuition is a signal. Don't dismiss it, but don't act on it without also pausing to evaluate what the evidence actually shows.

A Story from the Journey

I dated someone once who checked every box I thought I wanted. She was funny, sharp, confident. There was a current between us that I hadn't felt in years. There were signs early on — moments where she seemed put off by my custody schedule, times when she made comments that subtly suggested my kids were the reason we couldn't do things. I told myself those were just adjustment moments. I chose to believe the chemistry over the evidence.

Six months in, the relationship ended badly. And looking back, I can see every flag I ignored, lit up and waving. I wasn't ready to see them, so I didn't. Contrast that with a relationship that came later — quieter, slower, built on conversations more than sparks. She asked about my kids by name. She never made me feel like fatherhood was a problem to route around. When I had to change plans because of a school event, she said, "Of course — that's where you should be." Not every green light is dramatic. Most of them are just small, consistent moments of someone showing you who they are. I've learned to pay attention to those.

Dad Reflection

- Are there patterns I've noticed in someone I'm currently or recently dating that I've been rationalizing or minimizing?
- What specific behaviors would tell me — clearly and early — that someone genuinely respects my role as a father?
- Am I making decisions about who to date based primarily on chemistry, or am I also asking whether this relationship is good for my kids?

Takeaways

- Chemistry is real, but it can cloud judgment at exactly the moment when you need to see clearly.
- Red flags are patterns, not moments — watch for the consistent shape of someone's character over time.
- Green lights show up as small, consistent acts of respect, patience, accountability, and aligned values.
- The most important question isn't "Do I like her?" — it's "Is this good for me and my kids?"

Dad Challenge

Make two lists. On one side, write down the red flags you've observed — or ignored — in past relationships. On the other side, write down the green lights you're looking for, specifically as a dad. Post it somewhere private where you'll see it before a date. The goal isn't to be cynical — it's to be awake.

CHAPTER 11

Love, Legacy, and the Long View

"Love isn't just about the spark today — it's about the legacy you build for tomorrow."

There was a period after the divorce when I was convinced I would never let myself love again. Not in a dramatic, declarative way — just quietly, in the back of my chest, this low-level certainty that the kind of vulnerability love requires was a risk I was no longer willing to take. I had trusted, and it had cost me. I had opened myself fully, and I had been hurt in ways I didn't see coming. Why would I do that again?

But here's what I've learned: closing yourself off from love doesn't protect you. It just changes what you lose. Instead of risking heartbreak, you risk something quieter but equally serious — you risk a half-life. You risk showing up for your kids as a man who is present in body but closed in heart, who has carefully managed his exposure to anything that could hurt him again. And your kids see that. They feel it. They are learning from you, right now, every single day, what love looks like and what it costs.

Love after divorce is different. I won't pretend it isn't. It comes with baggage — not because you're broken, but because you've lived. It comes with caution and with scar tissue. It comes with the complexity of children who are still adjusting, and co-parenting dynamics, and a schedule that doesn't always leave room for romance. But different doesn't mean lesser. Love after divorce, when it comes, is often slower and more deliberate — built on substance rather than naivety, on choice rather than assumption. That's not a downgrade. That's maturity.

Your children are your first responsibility, and that doesn't change. But responsibility and joy are not opposites. You are allowed to experience love as a man, not just as a dad. You are allowed to be someone who receives affection, who has a partner, who builds something new. In fact, your kids benefit from seeing that. They need to know that loss does not have to be the last chapter — that the people they love most can recover, rebuild, and choose again. When they watch you love well, they are learning what healthy love looks like. That is an inheritance you can actually give them.

The long view means asking different questions. Not just "Is this fun right now?" but "What does this look like in five years?" Not "Does she make me feel good?" but "Do our values align in the ways that will matter when things get hard?" Shared values — around family, integrity, faith, finances, parenting, what a good life looks like — are not romantic, but they are the foundation. Chemistry fades and surges. Character stays. Choose character.

I think about the legacy I'm building for my kids when it comes to love. My son is watching how I treat women — whether I speak about them with respect, whether I keep my word, whether I walk away from relationships that don't honor us both. My daughter is watching what she should expect from a man — whether presence and kindness and patience are the standard, or whether they're the exception. Those lessons are not lectures. They are lived. They are watching me, right now. And that responsibility doesn't feel like a burden — it feels like a calling.

Practical Ways to Love with the Long View

- Align on values before you invest emotionally. Have real conversations about what matters — family, faith, finances, parenting philosophy. These conversations aren't unromantic; they're essential.

- Let your kids see healthy love in action. Not the performance of romance, but the everyday work of respect, patience, and partnership.
- Give yourself permission to open your heart again. Caution is wisdom, but permanent closure is a different kind of wound.
- Write a vision statement for the relationship you want. Not a checklist, but a picture: what does your life look like? What does your family feel like? What kind of love do you want your kids to grow up watching?
- Stay patient with the pace of real love. It often arrives quietly, without fanfare. Don't dismiss it because it doesn't feel like the fireworks you remember.

A Story from the Journey

I remember the first time I let myself fall for someone after the divorce — really let myself fall, not just enjoy someone's company. I was terrified in a way that surprised me. I kept waiting for the other shoe to drop. I kept looking for the moment when something would shatter. She was kind to me in a way that felt almost foreign. She was kind to my kids in a way that felt like watching something I'd been hoping for without knowing it.

It took a long time to stop bracing. But slowly, I did. And what I found on the other side of that fear was something I hadn't anticipated: I was stronger for loving again, not weaker. The part of me that had closed down after the divorce — the part that had decided love was too costly — came back. Not the naive version, but something more honest and more grounded. My kids grew up watching that relationship. My son told me once, when he was older, "I want something like you have, Dad." I thought about what he'd witnessed: the patience, the respect, the way we worked through disagreements without warfare. He didn't say he wanted fireworks. He said he wanted what he'd seen. That's the legacy. That's the whole thing.

Dad Reflection

- What fears are still keeping me at arm's length from the possibility of love? Are they protecting me, or are they costing me?
- What do I want my kids to learn about love from watching me — not what I tell them, but what they see?
- If I picture the relationship I want five years from now, what does it look like? What does it require of me to get there?

Takeaways

- Closing yourself off from love after divorce doesn't protect you — it limits you in ways that affect your kids too.
- Love after divorce is different — slower, more deliberate, built on substance — and that's a strength, not a deficit.
- Your children are learning what love looks like from watching you. You are building their blueprint right now.
- The long view favors shared values and character over chemistry and chemistry alone. Choose accordingly.

Dad Challenge

This week, write your vision for love. Not a dating profile — a real vision. What kind of relationship do you want your kids to witness? What kind of man do you want to be in love? What will you require of yourself and of the person you choose? Keep it somewhere you can return to. Let it be your compass.

Conclusion

Dating as a divorced dad is not about rushing to fill a silence or proving that you're still someone worth choosing. It's not about moving on or getting over what happened. It's about something harder and more meaningful than that: it's about growing. Growing into the man you want to be, showing up for your kids with everything you have, and — when the time is right — choosing love again with open eyes and an honest heart.

Everything in this book has pointed toward one thing: presence. Your children do not need you to be perfect. They do not need you to have the right answer about when to date or how to introduce someone or what love should look like. They need you to be there — emotionally available, honest, and willing to do the work. Presence is the foundation. Any healthy relationship you build must grow from that foundation, not replace it.

The road back to love after divorce is not a straight line. There will be false starts and moments of doubt. There will be nights when you wonder if you're getting it right, and mornings when you're proud of who you're becoming. Both are part of the journey. You don't need to arrive anywhere perfect — you just need to keep moving forward with intention.

You are not just a divorced man trying to date. You are a dad who is teaching his children what it looks like to fall down and get back up with dignity. You are showing them that love is worth trying again, that healing is possible, that integrity matters, that presence is everything. That is a profound gift — one that will outlast any single relationship and shape who your children become.

Keep showing up. Not perfectly. Just honestly, patiently, and fully. The road isn't easy, but it is absolutely worth it.

Acknowledgments

This book would not exist without the grace and patience of my children, who have taught me more about love and presence than any book ever could. To my family — thank you for never letting me forget what matters most. To the friends who sat with me in the hard seasons and refused to let me disappear into bitterness — you know who you are. And to every dad who picked this book up hoping for a little clarity in a confusing season: thank you for caring enough to look. The fact that you're reading means you're already doing it right.

About the Author

Brandon Antoni is a divorced father of two — a son and a daughter — who believes that presence, not perfection, is what kids need most from their dads. After walking through the pain of separation and divorce, Brandon committed to building stronger, healthier, and more intentional bonds with his children. His passion for fatherhood and integrity led him to write The Present Dad series, offering encouragement and guidance for dads at every stage of the journey. Brandon lives in the American Southwest and writes about what it means to choose your children — every day, on purpose.

The Present Dad Series

In Their Own Voices — What do kids actually think about divorce, about their dads, about the moments that mattered? This powerful companion volume gathers the perspectives of children who lived it — their fears, their questions, their deepest needs, and the things they wish their fathers had known. It is an unflinching and ultimately hopeful portrait of what kids need most, told in their words.

The Blended Dad — Building a healthy blended family is one of the most complex and rewarding challenges a dad can take on. This next book in The Present Dad Series walks through the real work of integrating households, honoring existing relationships, building new ones, and leading a blended family with patience, clarity, and love. Because a blended family isn't a consolation prize — it's a new beginning.

The Present Dad Series | Next Chapter Imprint

www.ingramcontent.com/pod-product-compliance
Lightning Source LLC
LaVergne TN
LVHW011051110826
845149LV00015B/3458

* 9 7 8 1 9 6 9 5 5 2 0 4 5 *